RENE PAPPONE

# THE HAI HONG

## PROFIT, TEARS AND JOY

HOW CANADA LED THE RESCUE OF 2,500
REFUGEES ABOARD A RUSTING FREIGHTER

## The Hai Hong: Profit, Tears and Joy

First published by Employment and Immigration Canada: 1982.

Revised and updated: 2015.

Photographs courtesy of Ian Hamilton.

Thanks also to the Toronto *Globe and Mail* for granting permission to reprint an article.

**The Hai Hong**:
Profit, Tears and Joy

ISBN   978-0-9783799-1-9

Cover and layout design: Mary Montague  m3m@rogers.com

Published by Rene Pappone

This book is available from
https://www.createspace.com/Products/Book/
In the *site* space select *store*, type in the title *The Hai Hong* and click the search icon.

# ACKNOWLEDGEMENTS

This book could not have been written without the generous assistance of several individuals who shared their knowledge about the *Hai Hong* crisis or made valuable comments on the manuscript: J.C. (Cal) Best, Ian Hamilton, Bud Cullen, Nicole Chenier Cullen, W. K. (Kirk) Bell, Ernest Allen, Bill Nauss, John Almeida, Bob Lefebvre, Thelma O'Connell, Mack Erb, Len Westerberg, Dan Doctor, Eva Ludwig, Doug Hill, Luu Dat Phuoc and Guy Ouellett.

Special appreciation is also due to Margaret Beare, Anita Rutledge, Valerie Raymond and Pierre Bourgeault for editing the original manuscript; and to Rose Simard, Linda Latour and Suzanne Cote for processing the original manuscript.

Thanks and appreciation to Michael and Jo Molloy, Michael McCormick, Ian Hamilton and Bonnie Boyle for assistance in updating the manuscript, and to Mary Montague for designing and formatting the second edition of this book.

*Looking back on this splendid operation, I remember being distinctly proud of the department and particularly of some individuals who dedicated so much of their time and energy to making it a success. Likewise the response of the Canadian people, the churches and service clubs was most heartwarming.*

Bud Cullen

Minister of Employment
and Immigration Canada
during the Hai Hong crisis.

# TABLE OF CONTENTS

# AUTHOR'S NOTE

This book, first published in 1982, was updated and revised to mark the 40th anniversary of the downfall of Saigon, April 30, 1975.

April 2015

# INTRODUCTION

Even though the flood of human cargo was rising with alarming speed, the world seemed incapable of comprehending the developments.

Three years had passed since the 1975 downfall of Saigon. The Vietnamese, fearful of a wretched existence in the so-called New Economic Zones, continued to stream toward the treacherous seas.

They were known as the "boat people," courageous individuals who stowed their meagre belongings on leaky vessels in what was often a vain and tragic search for freedom. At the time it was said that four out of every 10 refugees either did not survive the fury of the South China Sea or fell prey to the pirates who lurked there.

The more fortunate ones would endure these perils and the ravages of thirst and starvation and miraculously arrive on foreign shores, only to be greeted by hostile inhabitants whose countries were already buckling under the physical and financial burdens imposed by overcrowded refugee camps.

Whatever glimmer of hope the inhospitable beaches might have offered, it was quickly extinguished for many of the boat people. They soon cried out in anguish as their unreceptive hosts pushed their shattered vessels and dreams back to sea. And, the world seemed to turn a blind eye.

An unknown freighter, a rusting cargo ship that had been purchased for scrap, was to shock the world to attention. *The Hai Hong*, a 1,568-ton vessel constructed in 1948 and last registered in Panama, was the axis of a commercial venture that charged refugees for passage.

Amid reports of a dramatic increase in the number of refugees who were seeking escape from Vietnam, the *Hai Hong*, laden with some 2,500 Vietnamese refugees, dropped anchor off the Malaysian city of Port Klang in the Straits of Malacca on November 9, 1978.

The Malaysians refused to allow the *Hai Hong* passengers to disembark and the voyage became an international saga. For several tense days, the ship rode anchor and seemed headed for disaster until Canada launched a plan that spurred the world community into action.

Although the crisis was over a single boatload of people, the incident drew world attention to the magnitude of the refugee predicament in Southeast Asia. Less than a year later, Canada and 71 other countries pledged to increase their intakes of Vietnamese, Laotian and Cambodian refugees.

While the *Hai Hong* issue set off concerted world action to resolve a growing refugee crisis, I like to think that Canada's leadership in rescuing the boat's passengers was equally important. It was the marshalling point that set Canada on the road to the largest refugee resettlement operation in its history.

The focus of this book is the human drama that unfolded as Canada quickly began a rescue operation to end the atrocious suffering aboard the dilapidated ship.

# CHAPTER ONE

# MOUNTING PRESSURE

While many Ottawans accepted the late November snow flurries of 1978 as a prelude to challenging months on the ski slopes of the rolling Gatineau Hills, Ernest Allen worried about the chilly autumn air.

Allen's mind these days was half-way across the globe, in tropical Kuala Lumpur where temperatures hovered around 32 degrees Celsius. Canadian military aircraft would soon touch down in the humid Malaysian capital, just long enough to refuel and pick up 604 refugees from the *Hai Hong* freighter who had been selected for resettlement in Canada.

What bothered Allen, head of Canada Immigration's Asia-Pacific Bureau, was that these refugees were ill-equipped for the biting cold that would greet them 30 hours later at Montreal-Dorval International Airport, since renamed Montreal-Pierre Elliott Trudeau International Airport. Crammed aboard the old rusty freighter, they were poorly clad in light clothing, some barefoot and nearly exhausted after five weeks of benumbing boredom.

Allen was now spending most of his time on the complex plan to bring the refugees to Canada. "The pressures and concerns were related to trying to coordinate it, to put it all together, and making it stick together," Allen recalled.

In early November 1978 the veteran foreign service immigration officer had little inkling that he would be embroiled in such a large-scale rescue operation. The *Hai Hong*, then, was just a name that Allen saw as he scanned the heavy load of daily telex messages coming in from Southeast Asia.

"We had hoped the Malaysian government would allow the people to disembark," he said, but when the Malaysian authorities decided to tow the vessel back to sea it became obvious that if Canada was to do something positive it would have to be done quickly.

The *Hai Hong* entered centre stage just as the flow of refugees from Vietnam was escalating rapidly. The outflow began as a trickle following the defeat of Saigon in 1975, but by the fall of 1978 it had climbed from between 2,000 and 3,000 a month to an unprecedented level between 12,000 and 15,000 a month.

In 1978, Canada was conducting two refugee resettlement programs in Southeast Asia. The first program which started in January brought 50 families of Vietnamese small boat refugees to Canada each month. Under the second program, announced in September, Canada began accepting 20 Indochinese families a month from refugee camps in Thailand. Under these and previous special programs, about 8,500 Vietnamese had already come to Canada following the Communist victory in Vietnam three years earlier.

The growing number of people fleeing from Vietnam in late 1978 was an indication to Allen and his officers in Southeast Asia that Canada and other refugee-accepting countries would soon have to think about increasing their commitments to ease the growing misery.

These refugees were running from Communism, and the fear of the unknown life they would face if sent to the New Economic Zones. Young people feared military conscription, while those of Chinese origin were perturbed by a government decree which denounced them as traitors to Vietnam. "They were aware that the Vietnamese government was doing all in its power to get rid of them," said Allen. Some 150,000 to 200,000 of them had fled to China.

Life in a New Economic Zone was anything but pleasant, Allen noted. "It really means going off to untilled farmland, basically jungle, where people live without benefit of any housing. They must scrape to make a living . . . and acquire food either by growing it or by purchasing it on the black market." Medical drugs were not available and the death rate was high.

"Their funds or possessions had been taken over by the government," Allen added. "Really, they had nothing to live for."

Canada had encountered refugees from one other 'profit' ship before the *Hai Hong* came into the picture. In October 1978, the *Southern Cross* – carrying some 1,200 paying escapees, the majority of whom were ethnic Chinese – had landed in Indonesia and Canada accepted 81 persons for resettlement.

The first hint that the *Hai Hong* was on its way from Vietnam came in a telex which Allen received on November 6. It reported that the vessel had left Singapore on October 15, ostensibly bound for Hong Kong but that it was believed the ship anchored off the Mekong Delta and "took on a cargo of 2,000 plus" refugees. Not surprisingly, the telex noted that fragmentary reports indicated that the *Hai Hong* was "a profit-making venture."

Allen later remarked: "It is our belief that those who left on the *Hai Hong* had all paid, and paid rather handsomely, for a place aboard this very, very overcrowded ship."

Each refugee is believed to have paid 16 pieces of gold or $3,200 U .S. – 10 pieces for Vietnamese officials and six pieces for the promoters based in Singapore. It is estimated that the ship's Hong Kong owners pocketed between $2 million and $5 million for this 'humanitarian' voyage.

In addition, there was firm evidence that other profit venturing ships were already in the pipeline, and interviews with refugees revealed that Vietnamese authorities were permitting ethnic Chinese to leave Vietnam for a price.

The *Hai Hong* left the Mekong Delta on about October 24, after its passengers boarded her in broad daylight. The ship ran into Typhoon Rita and was forced toward Taramba Island in the Indonesian archipelago. It steamed from there toward Malaysia where it dropped anchor on November 9, just off Port Klang on the eastern side of the Malay peninsula.

For Malaysia, the human cargo of the *Hai Hong* represented an additional burden to an already onerous responsibility. Since 1975, more than 50,000 boat people had sought asylum on Malaysian territory and the arrivals far exceeded the numbers being resettled in other countries. Malaysia's refugee camps were bursting with some 35,000 people.

The Malaysian authorities feared that if the *Hai Hong* passengers were accommodated, other shiploads of refugees would soon arrive at her shores. So the government refused to allow the passengers to disembark, claiming that the *Hai Hong* was a commercial operation and arguing that, because money had changed hands, the Vietnamese could not be considered as refugees.

The United Nations High Commissioner for Refugees (UNHCR) and the international community, Canada included, shared Malaysia's concerns about commercialization. All wanted to assist the people without encouraging unscrupulous entrepreneurs to use human suffering for profit. The role of Vietnamese authorities in the massive exodus was also causing consternation.

The international dilemma was featured in a story which appeared in the November 9 issue of the *Asian Wall Street Journal*. It described the "mounting alarm" among governments and the diplomatic community in Southeast Asia over growing evidence of the "Vietnamese Role in Exodus of Refugees." The voyage of the *Hai Hong*, said the *Journal*, "offers best proof yet of active assistance" from Vietnamese officials.

The newspaper story, written by Raphael Pura and Barry Wain, said government ministries and diplomats "fear that the *Hai Hong's* voyage marks the opening of a new, potentially explosive chapter in the three-year-old drama of the refugee exodus . . ."

Canada's uneasiness stemmed from the fear that if the *Hai Hong* affair was not resolved properly, the refugee efforts in Southeast Asia could be thrown into disrepute. Immigration's Kirk Bell, Director General of

Recruitment and Selection, termed it "a problem that requires an international solution." Any unilateral action by Canada, he worried, could be counterproductive.

Canada stated publicly that it would be guided by policy decisions taken by the UNHCR and would support whatever stance the UN took as it led the diplomatic negotiations with Malaysian authorities.

Behind the scenes, however, Immigration Minister Bud Cullen and senior immigration officers were becoming increasingly apprehensive as events unfolded.

"At the outset, we were prepared to await the decision of the United Nations High Commissioner for Refugees," Cullen recalled.

"I wanted him to show some leadership and I did not want to usurp his role, but I was becoming very impatient and knew that we were not going to wait too long. We all knew without voicing it to one another that we were going to do something to take the leadership in resolving the problem."

Meanwhile, as the international community struggled to find a solution, the *Hai Hong* passengers waited anxiously in the suffocating heat aboard the 30-year-old freighter for some news about their uncertain future. The UNHCR adopted the position that the passengers were refugees and began to pressure the Malaysians to allow them to go ashore. This included a personal appeal from Poul Hartling, the United Nations High Commissioner for Refugees.

Around the world, newsroom teletypes soon began spewing out reports of the dreadful conditions and cramped quarters aboard the vessel, now surrounded by a flotilla of Malaysian warships, police launches and coast guard vessels in an ever-tightening ring of security.

One news report, carried by Reuters five days after the ship appeared off Malaysia, said that "the few reporters who have managed to board the *Hai Hong* described conditions on the ship as squalid." The dispatch, published November 14 in the Toronto *Globe and Mail,* quoted the reporters as saying some of the Vietnamese "were too weak to stand and open sores were common among the 1,280 children."

There were fears that an "epidemic could break out unless urgent medical attention was forthcoming," the story continued.

The early newspaper accounts of serious illness aboard the ship were unfounded. Medical and food supplies had been provided to the refugees by the UNHCR and the Red Crescent (Red Cross). However, the reports did help to create a realization that there was a serious refugee problem in Southeast Asia and to generate belated world sympathy.

In Canada, journalists began asking Canada Immigration about possible Canadian initiatives to end the plight of the *Hai Hong* people. In the House of Commons, Cullen told Members of Parliament that Canada was likely to be one of the first countries approached by the UN to help with the *Hai Hong* passengers.

"I continued to dance around the questions to some extent because of suggestions that we might consider refugees who had relatives in Canada, or those with 'promise of visa' letters which had been handed out in Vietnam before the Americans pulled out," Cullen related. "However, we decided to leave the door open, indicating that we were prepared to look at any eventuality, depending upon what action and what reports we had from the United Nations."

*The Canadian Press,* meanwhile, carried a dispatch from Port Klang, announcing that "the Malaysian government decided Wednesday to force a freighter packed with 2,500 Vietnamese, mostly ethnic Chinese, to leave its territorial waters." The Malaysians would assist in repairing the ship's engine and supply the passengers with food, water and medicine but they remained firm in their stance that the people aboard the vessel were not genuine refugees.

ABC Television reporter Bill Redeker, who spent 15 minutes aboard the *Hai Hong*, was quoted in the story as saying there was filth everywhere and that the refugees had hardly enough room to sleep. Redeker said most of the babies on board were suffering and that many people were sick.

The reports about the *Hai Hong* led the Toronto *Star* to cry out editorially on November 15 that "Asian refugees must be helped." The newspaper denounced the callous attitude of man's inhumanity to man, pointing out that the "flight from Vietnam has become a tidal wave, involving more than a third of a million frightened human beings." In face of the heavy flow of refugees from Vietnam as well as from Cambodia, Bangladesh and China, the "world has remained largely unmoved," the *Star* lamented.

A majority of the telex messages that poured into External Affairs and Canada Immigration headquarters from Southeast Asia during the week of November 12 bore the signature of Ross Francis, Canada's High Commissioner in Kuala Lumpur. He was accompanying the UNHCR representative in the discussions with the Malaysians in an attempt to resolve the Hai Hong situation. Two of his messages would set off a series of events that would mount a speedy program to give some of the *Hai Hong* passengers safe haven in Canada.

The first message, November 16, contained a distressing passage confirming reports that the Malaysians intended to tow the disabled ship out to sea. By then her engines had been made inoperable by the Vietnamese refugees aboard the ship, some of whom had been quoted as saying they would rather die than return home.

Malaysia's decision to tow the ship out to sea came as a real jolt to Cullen. "I felt that Malaysia was calling our bluff and heaven knows they had every right to, having accepted something in excess of 35,000 refugees." As immigration officer Allen reflected: "The news was the turning point for us."

After another meeting with the Malaysians the following day, Francis rushed word to Ottawa that the Malaysians had indicated willingness to transmit a message to their Prime Minister recommending that they delay forcing the *Hai Hong* to sea long enough to give the UNHCR and other countries time to make resettlement arrangements. "If the Prime Minister agrees, UNHCR and recipient countries, including Canada, will have to take immediate action to interview the passengers and remove them from Malaysia," said Francis.

That, said Allen, was the signal for interested countries "to do something special." The Malaysians, he continued, seemed to be saying "fine, if you want something to happen, you take the first step."

Canada's eagerness to help was tempered by the strain of a moral dilemma. Thousands of refugees who had languished for some time in Malaysian refugee camps were still awaiting resettlement and "I wondered whether, in this instance, we should give priority to people on the *Hai Hong* who had just arrived," Cullen said.

As the tone of the messages between Ottawa and Kuala Lumpur reached a critical note, Quebec Immigration Minister Jacques Couture told the Quebec National Assembly on November 15 that his province would be willing to accept some of the refugees. Two days later the Quebec government formally told Cullen that the province would be willing to accept at least 200

*Hai Hong* refugees or 30 per cent of the number Canada accepted, if that number exceeded 200.

"Jacques and I had developed quite a good friendship and a very trusting relationship," Cullen noted. He described the Quebec gesture as "the first real break" for Canada's imminent involvement in helping to end the suffering aboard the *Hai Hong*.

"Fortunately, the media were pushing both me and the department in the very direction that we wanted to go by constantly asking us what we intended to do," said Cullen. Members of Parliament, too, kept up their questioning in the House of Commons and telegrams and letters from the public flowed into the department.

On November 17 there was another development. The *Associated Press,* filing from Geneva, reported that the United States had joined with Canada and France in offering to help resettle the stranded *Hai Hong* refugees.

# CHAPTER TWO

# DAY OF DECISION

There was no doubt in Allen's mind that Friday morning, November 17, as he hurried along the second-floor corridor of the Bourque Building which housed Immigration headquarters in Ottawa. Allen was heading toward Kirk Bell's office where he would meet with Bell and Douglas Hill, an External Affairs officer seconded to Immigration as Director, Refugee Policy. The three men had been spending more and more time together in the last few days analysing the daily developments in Malaysia.

Hill was just beginning to get the feel of his new job when the *Hai Hong* made the scene. "Up until then, I had only dealt with policy formulation," he recalled. "Suddenly, it was the real thing."

Bell's empathy toward the plight of the refugees aboard the aging vessel stemmed from both his knowledge of shipboard living – acquired as a deckhand aboard Great Lakes freighters – and a strong desire to avoid repetition of the pitiful voyages made by German Jews who, in the 1930s, paid to get out of Nazi Germany and consequently were not well received by many countries.

Cullen, however, had dismissed any concerns about the fact that the *Hai Hong* refugees had paid money to leave their country. "Many Jewish people in the Second World War had paid to get out of Europe . . . but most assuredly they were refugees warranting and needing help." He felt the same about the *Hai Hong* refugees. In his mind the only questions were how many *Hai Hong* refugees should Canada take and "how do we make the selection?"

Remembering the hot summer days he spent aboard Great Lakes freighters, Bell comprehended the discomfort of the *Hai Hong* passengers. "I can tell you that on a hot day (on deck) you can burn the soles of your feet right through your shoes. Imagine being there (on the *Hai Hong*) 24 hours a day with little protection from the elements and no room for you below!" Not that the holds of the ship would offer much comfort. "They can be really hot too," he added.

The problems aboard ship were compounded because, unlike the small boats which carried refugees from Vietnam, big vessels such as the *Hai Hong* carried a large number of children and elderly people.

Bell explained that "people took advantage of the relatively more secure situation of a big boat to come with a total family. Often you would find three generations of people aboard." So he worried that the confinement would be a greater ordeal and much more of a health hazard for the young and elderly. "The risk of an epidemic was very real," he said.

Bell, Allen and Hill came to a quick conclusion at the hastily-called meeting on November 17. "We had to decide what offer of assistance we would make," Bell said. If the refugees could not get off the ship "it could very well be the end of them."

The three officers agreed on two thrusts: first, the Malaysians had to be stopped from towing the disabled vessel out to sea; and second, Canada would have to make a commitment of such magnitude that other countries would be encouraged to follow.

"We felt that if we could help enough of them, we could help them all" because other countries would likely follow Canada's lead, said Bell. "I've seen a number of refugee crises (where) everyone wants to help but they're afraid to commit themselves for fear they will be caught with the whole thing," he added. "People hold back from making first commitments."

Canadian experience, however, gave Bell a great deal of confidence. Canada led the way in taking political prisoners from Chile, in helping stranded East European refugees in Belgium and France, and in accepting people during the Cyprus conflict. "In every instance, we found that we did not have to go it alone," said Bell.

While the three officers did not come up with a specific figure for the number of refugees Canada should accept, there was general agreement that it should be in the neighbourhood of 250 to 350. Bell then met with J .C. (Cal) Best, Executive Director, Immigration and Demographic Policy, and Jack Manion, Chairman, Canada Employment and Immigration Commission.

"It was in my final discussion with the Chairman that the figure of 600 was hit upon as being the right number," recalled Bell. This figure represented about 25 per cent of the number of refugees aboard the ship and "we felt it would have a positive impact on the Malaysians and encourage other countries to join."

Manion then called the Minister, who was attending a political convention in Toronto, and proposed that Canada accept 600 *Hai Hong* passengers. Cullen reacted positively: "I was satisfied, after Jack's briefing, that this was a reasonable figure and that as a government we could afford it."

In ordinary circumstances, Cullen would have brought the matter before Cabinet for discussion, but in view of the urgency he advised the Prime Minister, Pierre Trudeau, verbally and spoke to Robert Andras, his predecessor, the President of the Treasury Board, about the possible requirement for additional money. External Affairs, meanwhile, briefed its Minister – Don Jamieson – who was in Eastern Canada for a speaking engagement.

As the pieces began to fall into place, External Affairs advised Canada's High Commissioner to Malaysia, Ross Francis, that "Ministerial consideration (is) being given for admitting 600 refugees aboard the *Hai Hong* to Canada as special response to urgency of situation. Final decision will be made November 18 morning Ottawa time."

Allen began to get his people into place. He requested the Immigration office in Hong Kong to send an officer to Kuala Lumpur to assist in selecting the refugees, warning that "we anticipate need to move those selected within a brief period of time."

The job went to 22-year-old Scott Mullin, a native of Halifax, who had been posted to Hong Kong only one month earlier as part of his foreign service training program. "He was fast on his feet and did a fantastic job," said Allen.

Francis, meanwhile, alerted Immigration's Ian Hamilton and Richard Martin in Singapore to remain on standby to go to Kuala Lumpur during the weekend if necessary.

The selection had to be done rapidly so that the refugees could be moved to Canada with a minimum of delay. Timing was critical if the Canadian team was to maintain its credibility with Malaysian officials. While Ernest Allen contacted Health and Welfare Canada (HWC) and the RCMP to arrange for on-the-spot medical and security examinations, Jack Manion called the Department of National Defence (DND) to request its support and assistance in arranging transportation and a reception area for the refugees on their arrival in Canada.

The evacuation outline and proposals for settlement were discussed late Friday afternoon when a dozen immigration officials met to map out a strategy for bringing the refugees to Canada within a week.

Nicole Chenier, Minister Bud Cullen's executive assistant, told the group that Cullen was prepared to hold a news conference the following morning in Toronto to announce the program.

"I must admit, however, that I was apprehensive," said Cullen. The department had moved quickly to "get everything together . . . and to brief me on all of the salient features of the operation." However, the news conference would take place during the course of a political convention in Toronto and "I was concerned that to any reporters, cynical or not, it might very well appear to be a bit of political hokery-pokery."

Pressure, too, was felt by Bill Nauss, Director of Settlement. He had to ensure that the refugees did not suffer from the harsh climate upon their arrival in Canada.

Bell saw a need for community involvement. "I was particularly anxious about the *Hai Hong* operation because it obviously was not going to be the end of the road," he said. The entire situation in Southeast Asia demanded more effort and public support if Canada was to increase her involvement. The *Hai Hong* situation, said Bell, was a "way of personalizing the tragedy in Indochina for the Canadian public."

A subsequent call on the Canadian public for assistance brought an overwhelming response in terms of material and volunteer help for the *Hai Hong* refugees. And it provided the impetus for Cullen to announce (on December 22) a new program for Canada to accept 5,000 Indochinese refugees in 1979.

The Hai Hong affair had a further repercussion. It stimulated the refugee sponsorship program which had remained largely dormant since it was introduced in the new Immigration Act which came into effect on April 10, 1978.

"The (sponsorship) program took on a new dimension," said Bell, and in early 1979 several church groups came forward to discuss the refugee crisis and, as a result, signed national sponsorship agreements with the Canada Employment and Immigration Commission (CEIC). This, in turn, led to a government decision in the summer of 1979 to accept up to 50,000 refugees over two years on a shared basis with private sponsors.[1]

Cullen faced a somewhat skeptical group of reporters at his Toronto news conference on Saturday, November 18, and he remembers his nervousness. "Never did a Minister finish reading a prepared text and

[1] The target of bringing 50,000 Indochinese refugees to Canada in 1979 and 1980 was eventually increased by 10,000.

look up with as much concern as I did on that particular occasion," he said.

Bell, who had briefed the Minister beforehand, shared Cullen's uneasiness. "I don't know what they (the media) were thinking exactly. I think they saw this as a capital P political gesture . . . as a way to get out in front."

Once the questioning started, however, the reporters "became interested and emotionally involved," Bell observed. "I have never been at a news conference when the press started off with one train of mind and then totally turned around."

As the emotional aspects of the story unfolded, reporters began to stand and crowd around Cullen. They, like the Employment and Immigration officers who would have to deal with the refugees, worried about selection, the cold, and whether Canada's gesture would really bring other countries on board.

Whatever the emotions, their stories seemed to electrify their editors. The Toronto *Sun* ran a story on Sunday, November 19 under the headline "Canada first to offer haven," and noted that the Immigration department had sent telegrams to the provinces seeking homes for the refugees. The CBC invited Cullen to appear on its Sunday evening radio program, *Cross Canada Checkup*, where he pushed for public assistance.

On Sunday, Allen sent a telex to Hamilton, who was now in Kuala Lumpur, telling him to "immediately commence the selection of up to 600 persons" from the *Hai Hong*.

"You are to have the first group of approximately 200 ready for departure by mid-week, and pending the DND decision (concerning aircraft availability) you should block off space aboard commercial carriers," Allen advised Hamilton.

"In view of reported medical problems suffered by refugees would appreciate having the initial reaction of commercial airlines as to their willingness to carry," he added. "If not already considered, you should seek assistance of Red Cross or other like organization in providing refugees destined to Canada with winter weight clothing."

# CHAPTER THREE

# PREPARATIONS ABROAD

When Hamilton arrived in Malaysia from Singapore on Saturday, he was unaware of the type of operation Cullen would announce. He was under the impression that Canada would select about 200 refugees and "in terms of documentation, the time available and personal effects, we were equipped for a three- or four-day effort."

Francis, Hamilton and Richard Martin spent the weekend in a round of meetings and telephone calls with the Malaysians and the UNHCR, as well as with the Americans and the French who were prepared to accept some of the *Hai Hong* refugees. The Australians took part in the discussions but had declined from the outset to become involved in selecting any of the refugees for resettlement.

Canada's decision to accept the *Hai Hong* refugees was "received with mixed emotions by the other countries," said Hamilton. His personal feeling was that the Malaysians were very serious about towing the vessel out to sea. "I had seen other boats turned away. Why not the *Hai Hong*?"

The Malaysians had made it clear that none of the *Hai Hong* people would be permitted to remain in Malaysia. They were determined to dissuade similar commercially-motivated enterprises, and refused to facilitate Canada's selection of the *Hai Hong* passengers who, they maintained, were not legitimate refugees. The Canadians would not be permitted to board the ship, nor could the refugees set foot on Malaysian soil.

The parties, however, reached a compromise: the selection interviews would take place aboard a small Malaysian police launch mid-way between the shore and the ship. (The Malaysians later changed their minds and used a minesweeper). And, to lessen the risk of an accident, the interviews would take place between dawn and dusk while the seas were light.

Canada would have little control over who was to be interviewed. A message from Kuala Lumpur to Ottawa, describing the situation a few days later, explained that Canada's priorities had to be relayed to the Vietnamese via Malaysian police officers.

The Canadians had always hoped that if they could make satisfactory arrangements for selection and transportation, the Malaysians would allow them to board the *Hai Hong*. "The Malaysians were interested in our plans and, in fact, they suggested that we take all of them (the refugees)," said Hamilton. He felt the Malaysian authorities may have been concerned about the rejection of any of the refugees by third countries. They wanted all of them out of Malaysia quickly and kept asking Hamilton: "How much time do you need?"

The questioning and the hard-line position of the Malaysians were enough to convince Hamilton that it would be quite a challenge for Canada to pull off the operation. "Our arrangements, therefore, were purposely over-planned so that nothing would go wrong." But there were more questions than answers, said Hamilton. "Where were we going to keep the selected refugees? How were we going to feed them? How could we deal with any medical problems?"

Ken Lewis, second secretary at the Canadian High Commission, Kuala Lumpur, and Bob Hayes, the Commission's administrative officer, would become Hamilton's miracle workers. "Ken never flinched when I began listing the things I needed – from an electrical generator and transportation to electric and portable typewriters, tables and chairs." By Monday, the High Commission looked like a warehouse. "It was a mess," Hamilton laughed. "Ken later told me that he thought I was crazy."

Hamilton, meanwhile, asked Datum Ruby Lee of the Red Crescent Society (Red Cross) in Malaysia to find some winter clothing for the refugees. "Mr. Hamilton, there is no winter here," she reminded him. The request, however, did not go unanswered. Several days later, when the refugees began arriving in Kuala Lumpur for the special flights to Canada, bales of sweaters appeared at the airport. All of the bales bore the Red Crescent label.

The initial meetings with Malaysian Security Police were difficult, Hamilton said. "They spoke to us in a demanding way and set up stringent security precautions never seen before." Steel-helmeted riot police, many of them armed with automatic weapons, appeared on the streets. Women members of the police carried canisters of mace. "It was their way of demonstrating that these (refugees) were dangerous, unwanted people who must be swept away."

Undaunted, the immigration officer began getting together a collection of Canadian souvenirs – principally flags and lapel pins – to establish the Canadian presence. And these articles soon began to appear on the streets. Some of the female security police even wore the maple leaf pins as earrings.

More Canadians began arriving in Kuala Lumpur during the weekend. The Canadian selection team now consisted of Hamilton, Scott Mullin, borrowed from Hong Kong, and Martin, along with the Quebec Immigration Service's Florent Fortin. They would be accompanied on the minesweeper by Lewis and Art Hamm, RCMP liaison officer. The on-the-spot medicals would be handled by Dr. J. David Holbrook of Health and Welfare Canada who, although ill, flew in from Singapore. Also on the team: an International Committee for European Migration photographer, two International Committee of the Red Cross documentation officers, and three women whose work Hamilton would later praise. They were Miss Low Pee Hong, a typist from Singapore, who was on a plane to Kuala Lumpur with notice of only three hours; Miss S. Szuniewycz, Canadian High Commission, Kuala Lumpur, who appeared for duty a few hours after a post-midnight call; and Miss F.N. Salleh, a locally-engaged typist at the High Commission in Kuala Lumpur, who would work "through to sunset although very seasick."

When it was over, Hamilton said of the three women: "None of them, I am sure, were advised when joining our service that they might become involved in such an extraordinary undertaking or be asked to work, as they did very well, under these conditions."

Hamilton was able to obtain a partial list of the *Hai Hong* passengers who had been documented by Malaysian authorities. Most of them indicated they had relatives or connections in the United States or Australia. There were about 50 cases involving 120 people who claimed Canadian connections ranging from close relatives to friends. There was some question about whether Canada could reach the 600 goal, but Hamilton told Ottawa in a telex Monday, November 20, that the team was ready to go on a moment's notice.

A heavy downpour greeted the Canadian team at 4 a.m. on November 21 as their cavalcade of trucks and cars left Kuala Lumpur for Port Klang to begin the selection interviews. "I still didn't know what kind of interview facilities would be available," Hamilton said. They had only been told by the Malaysians that they would not be permitted to board the *Hai Hong* because they said there was a danger they would be taken hostage.

When the immigration team arrived at Port Klang, they loaded their equipment aboard a police launch and pinned red bands on their sleeves. "These bands were given to us, for whatever reason, by the Malaysian security police," Hamilton explained. "I asked one of them, with tongue in cheek, whether the bands had any political significance!" There was no answer.

The Canadians received a courteous but somewhat cautious reception when the police launch and the flotilla of security boats reached the Malaysian minesweeper *Brinchang* that would serve as the temporary immigration processing centre. "The captain welcomed us but no one came forward to help us transfer our equipment to the minesweeper," Hamilton noted.

However, the captain did express dismay when he saw the generator and the gasoline to power it come aboard his ship. "He told us we couldn't use it because it was too dangerous," said Hamilton. The immigration officer began using some friendly persuasion to allay the captain's fears. "The ship's power is 220 DC and we need the generator to produce 220 AC so that we can run our typewriters," he explained. The captain reluctantly agreed to allow the equipment on board but directed that it be placed at the stern of the vessel.

"This meant that the generator would have to sit out in the open, in the rain." complained Hamilton. However, the "miles" of extension cords that Ken Lewis had brought along came in handy, allowing the team to assemble under a make-shift tent at the bow and connect to the generator at the rain-drenched stern.

Hamilton, whose hobbies include mechanics, was soaking wet from the heavy downpour as he attempted to start the generator. "I was on my hands and knees, pulling and pulling on the starter," he said. "It just wouldn't start." Finally, he located the problem: a wet ignition and a loose wire. "Imagine trying to dry the ignition under those conditions!"

Hamilton put the pieces back into place and gave the starter another pull, then another. It finally roared into action.

The Canadian team could see the *Hai Hong*, anchored about a mile away, but still had no word about the next move. Curious about what was happening aboard the freighter, they found a pair of binoculars and tried to survey the vessel, but a Malaysian police officer confiscated the binoculars before they could get more than a glimpse.

"We could see the *Hai Hong* but had no idea whether anyone wanted to come to Canada," Hamilton worried. He felt that the passengers would probably want to go to the United States. "I gave a stack of OS8s (immigration application forms) to the Malaysian police and asked them to hand out the documents on the *Hai Hong*."

# CHAPTER FOUR

# A REFUGEE'S STORY

Luu Dat Phuoc was one of the 2,500 refugees aboard the *Hai Hong*. He was among the first Vietnamese who descended the ship's ladder when the first police launch arrived on Tuesday, November 21 to ferry refugees to the minesweeper for immigration interviews. His ability to speak English, French, Vietnamese and Chinese made him a valuable member of the floating community, and he would act as one of the spokespersons.

Luu had been a businessman in Saigon, renamed Ho Chi Minh City after the 1975 Communist victory, where he operated an import-export business and an insurance company. He was also a commercial representative for several companies such as Alcan and Allied Chemical. Business would not last long, however.

"The Communists confiscated all banks and insurance companies and big companies like importers and exporters," he said. Bank accounts were frozen.

"They took everything."

Because of his business dealings with foreigners, Luu said he was "visited by police several times and taken to the police station for questioning." When the police pressure mounted in 1978, Luu decided it was time to leave.

Escape, however, would not be easy or without penalty. Two attempts by members of the family to escape Vietnam ended in failure and some of them spent four-month terms in the jungle camps, the New Economic Zones. "There is almost nothing to eat in those camps," said Luu, and the long work days would drive a person to physical exhaustion.

His desire to flee Vietnam with his whole family was tempered by the knowledge that if all of them were caught and sentenced to the camps, they would face extreme hardship. None of the family would be on the outside to supply the detainees with food and other necessities. For this reason, he decided to send his wife and children away in September; he would stay behind.

Luu had not heard from his family in the more than two months since he had spirited them out of Vietnam and onto a large ship, the *Southern Cross*. He only knew that because his wife, five daughters and son did not show up in a concentration camp in Vietnam, they had probably made it to safety. Somewhere.

Once he was convinced that they were safe, Luu made his own travel arrangements, boarded a small fishing boat, and after five days of a seasick voyage, boarded the *Hai Hong*.

"Conditions aboard the Hai Hong were terrible," he recalled. "There were too many people and little food or drinking water." His accommodation consisted of just enough space on deck to lie down, exposed to the rain and wind. The rain, he said, was worse than the heat.

The ship and its passengers were lucky enough to survive Typhoon Rita, but two old women died during the storm from illness and lack of food. "At one time, we feared all the old people and children would also die," Luu added.

When the *Hai Hong* arrived in Indonesia, the authorities refused to allow the passengers to land but did provide them with food and water. "They said they had made arrangements by radio to a warship at sea that was ready to allow us to go aboard."

The *Hai Hong* left Indonesia but after several days at sea, the warship had not appeared. "The food and water were almost depleted, and the people began fighting amongst each other," Luu said. The captain decided to go to Malaysia.

A BBC newscast reporting that France and Canada would accept some of the refugees spread quickly through the *Hai Hong*. Luu's hopes were high.

As other police launches ringed a security screen around the *Hai Hong*, the police launch carrying Luu and others in the first group of refugees to be interviewed by the Canadian team headed towards the Malaysian minesweeper *Brinchang* which tugged at its anchor in the choppy sea a mile away.

# CHAPTER FIVE

# SELECTION BEGINS

The Canada Immigration selection team perspired profusely in the stifling heat as the first police ferry left the *Hai Hong* for the *Brinchang*. The ferry operation had been delayed six hours by the Malaysians, cutting sharply into the time available for the first day of interviews. No explanation was ever given for the delay.

"The lull caused a great deal of tension," said Hamilton. The police launch that had gone out to the *Hai Hong* was kept hidden behind the freighter "so we had no idea about what was happening." Hamilton knew that Canada and the international community were monitoring the operation closely, yet he had no control over events. "This was Canada's opportunity to show leadership and I didn't want to let it slip by. We also knew that National

Defence was preparing the (Boeing) 707s for the airlift and that they would be arriving soon."

The interview area, rigged under a Bofors 40mm anti-aircraft gun on the cramped bow of the minesweeper, offered little comfort. A canvas cover provided some protection from the sun, but the unbearable heat and humidity sapped the team's energy. The sickening fumes from the generator and other vessels tied alongside drifted over the bow. Dr. Holbrook began administering medication as the rough seas added to the team's misery.

Hamilton had made one major decision about the selection procedures. No one under 12 years of age would be asked to make the trip between the *Hai Hong* and the minesweeper. The rough sea made the transfer operation too dangerous for children.

Suddenly, the police launch appeared from behind the *Hai Hong* and headed toward the minesweeper. "We expected the launch to be filled with passengers but when it came alongside there were only about eight people in the boat," Hamilton said. He was relieved when told that the initial group consisted of leaders from the refugee ship.

The next hour is now only a blur in Hamilton's mind. Anxious to get on with the selection interviews, "I grabbed the second refugee who came on board and began peppering him with questions."

"Do you speak English?"

"Yes."

"How many people want to come to Canada?"

"A lot."

Those last two words gave Hamilton new hope. "I want you to help me out and be our spokesman aboard the *Hai Hong*," Hamilton said excitedly. The man agreed but laughed heartily when he was told the Malaysians feared the Canadians would be held hostage if they boarded the freighter.

The refugee, Hamilton soon learned, was Luu Dat Phuoc whose family had disappeared two months earlier. "He had no idea where they were," Hamilton said. "I'm not sure what we said during our conversation, but I vaguely recalled that Luu told me that he had a wife and five daughters."

This information jogged the immigration officer's memory. In one of the refugee camps in Indonesia, Hamilton had called on three young women to help out with interpretations because they spoke excellent English, French, Chinese and Vietnamese. Their mother, two other sisters and a brother were in the same camp.

"There was a noticeable wetness in Luu's eyes and he trembled with joy when I told him that I knew the whereabouts of his family," Hamilton reminisced. Luu never forgot the day when Hamilton told him that "your family has already been accepted to go to Canada."

Hamilton promised that if Luu returned to the *Brinchang* the following day he would show him photographs of his daughters. The photos were among the personal possessions and identification documents that Hamilton had not been able to drop off in Singapore. "I had been travelling so much that I still had those photographs with me."

A mob of reporters greeted the Canadians when they returned to Port Klang at the end of the first day and announced that Canada had accepted 74 refugees, 25 of whom would go to Quebec. Hamilton provided the reporters with details of the operation, and then retired with his companions to the Port View Restaurant for a meal. The red arm bands that the Canadians had been ordered to wear soon began to upset other patrons in the restaurant. "The owner came over and asked us to take them off because their clients associated the bands with Communists."

The Canadian team returned to Kuala Lumpur that night and worked into the early hours of the following day. There was paperwork to complete and logistical details to work out for the airlift to Canada. What little sleep they got was interrupted by reporters who called them during the night at the Equitorial Hotel for information. "I eventually had to take the phone off the hook," said Hamilton.

The short rest was interrupted by a morning call. "Martin was a heavy sleeper, so I had asked him to leave his door open so that I could wake him up," Hamilton said. When he entered the room, Martin got out of bed "but I think he was still fast asleep. After I gave him some important instructions, he asked me to repeat them. I was so exhausted that I couldn't remember them myself."

The Canadian team boarded another minesweeper Wednesday morning, prepared for a full day of interviews. A telex outlining that day's activities contained some distressing news. "Chaos on the *Hai Hong* frequently prevents Vietnamese with Canadian connections from muscling their way t o *Hai Hong* launch transfer point." The decision not to interview young children was a good one.

The immigration officers, however, were determined that no relatives of Canadian residents would be left behind. The Malaysians agreed to take a loudhailer to the *Hai Hong* and ask Vietnamese with Canadian connections to identify themselves.

There was a note of pride in Martin's voice late Wednesday, November 22 when he telephoned Ernest Allen in Ottawa to report the team had selected 356 people. Combined with the previous day's selection of 74, Canada now had 430 people in process.

"We're going to finish tomorrow and then the problem is going to switch over to logistics of air transport," said Martin. The refugees would fly to Canada aboard the military707s.

The fatigue had left Hamilton punchy, and there was a noticeable strain in his voice when he took the receiver from Martin and began talking to Allen about the travel plans. The refugees, Hamilton was told, would have to be at the airport three hours ahead of takeoff in order to load the aircraft and proceed through the usual passenger screening.

"Listen, no!" exclaimed Hamilton. "They won't stand for this. These people haven't had a bath in a month and they've been pleading to me 'can't you do something?'"

The Malaysian police had ordered tight security for the ground transportation from Port Klang pier to the airport. The Malaysians claimed they were "afraid of incidents more on the part of the Malaysians than the refugees," so there would be an armed escort with the main roads sealed off. The refugees would be held on the buses until they reached the airport.

"No wash. No nothing," Hamilton said in disgust.

As the selection process was taking place off Port Klang, a group of settlement officers in Canada began laying the groundwork for receiving the refugees. National Defence had agreed to provide the Longue Pointe military camp as the staging area and by mid-week, military, government, and civilian personnel were busy transforming part of the base into a reception centre for the refugees.

Hamilton's information telexes to Ottawa and the manifests for each flight would contain information to help determine clothing sizes so that properly fitting outfits would be immediately available for the refugees upon arrival at Longue Pointe. "Shoes are another thing," advised Hamilton. "Everyone is either barefoot or in sandals."

"We'll arrange that," said Allen, instructing Hamilton to send copies of telexes to the Director of

Immigration and to Bob Lefebvre, who was in charge of the staging area at Longue Pointe.

"Sure, I remember him," interrupted Hamilton, "from when I was doing this in . . . " There was a brief pause before Allen jumped in. "Uganda," he prompted.

"Well, wherever I was before," Hamilton replied, his voice weary.

No serious medical health problems were evident among the refugees, although Dr. Holbrook thought one of them may have had a rheumatic heart problem and one woman had fractured an ankle in a fall.

Meanwhile, the UNHCR had approached Canada about taking three refugees with moderately severe burns. Since the Canadian selection team had not been able to board the *Hai Hong*, Hamilton had no way of determining their condition.

According to his information, a boiler had exploded and the refugees "were burned seriously enough that they are flat on their backs and were being given plasma." However, Hamilton noted that Dr. Holbrook had been told by the Malaysian medical team that the burns were superficial. There was never a clear explanation of the explosion.

Allen did not want to take any chances in the event that the burns were serious. He advised Hamilton that he would ask DND whether facilities were available aboard the aircraft to carry the burn victims. He would also speak to Health and Welfare about treatment immediately upon arrival in Canada.

Hamilton was pleased with the results of the second day of interviews. "We've taken the oldest refugee who is 82, and part of a large family, and we have taken the youngest refugee who was born aboard the boat." However, the scene aboard the minesweeper was depressing. "It's a very sad situation," Hamilton told Allen. "There are a lot of tearful sort of scenes."

The Canadian team had tried desperately to buoy the sagging spirits of the refugees by keeping conversations light. And the lunch boxes which the Canadians brought with them soon became common property. "When we tried to eat something, the refugees would stare at us. So, we offered to share our lunches."

Hamilton recalled one incident when an orange was given to a young Vietnamese mother. "She immediately gave it to her child but the child just stared at it, not knowing what it was." The mother wept.

During their telephone conversation, Allen wondered about the chances of reaching 600. "I think there will be no problem," Hamilton replied, adding that he felt confident now that 430 refugees had been selected.

"We should try to reach the 600, if possible," Allen said. "I rather like the idea of including the three persons who suffered the burns and I will work on that this morning."

There was a black mark on the newspages that day. Another boat, overcrowded with more than 200 refugees, was denied permission to dock and sank in the fast-flowing Trenganu River, about 500 kilometres northeast of Kuala Lumpur. More than half her passengers drowned. The Canadians and the UNHCR, said Hamilton, received the news in "sort of stunned silence."

On the following day, the telephone conversation between Allen and Hamilton was an excited one.

"We did it," exclaimed Hamilton. "We got 604."

"Excellent. Well done," congratulated Allen.

"The burn people turned out to be a big scare," said Hamilton. "They were very, very minor burns."

The scare exemplified the predicament that the Canadians faced in assessing second-hand information about conditions aboard the *Hai Hong*. "The whole exercise down here has been a little bizarre, a little distorted because we have not been allowed aboard the ship," Hamilton stressed.

Some of the refugees bound for Canada were suffering from injuries, Hamilton said, but his thoughts switched in mid-sentence, focussing instead on a tragedy that struck a family aboard the *Hai Hong*. "I think I spoke last night about a woman who had a fall and was killed. We took the entire family with the head of the family . . . a minor child of 17 with a relative in Vancouver."

The mother had completed the application form on behalf of her family before she died in the fall aboard the *Hai Hong*.

A broken leg seemed to be the major extent of the injuries among the refugees. There was the normal "garden variety" of medical ailments, said Hamilton. There were no stretcher cases among the people destined to Canada.

"Has the girl with the broken leg had it set in a cast?" Allen asked.

"No. She has not. It probably will need to be re-broken and reset, according to the doctor."

"OK, I'll pass it along to DND so they'll be aware of it."

Hamilton was becoming apprehensive about the interpretations of his telexes by headquarters. "I think anything I say about broken legs or skin rashes develops into major proportions," he worried.

"Not really," replied Allen. "It's just a matter for them (DND) to be prepared for it."

The Canadian team felt frustrated about not being able to inspect conditions aboard the *Hai Hong*, so Hamilton made a last request to the Malaysians before going to shore. "I told them, look, we've worked very hard. We've taken more than 600 people. Could we go close by the *Hai Hong*?"

The Malaysians agreed and shortly afterward the Canadian team sailed by the slightly listing vessel. "As we went by the boat – this old, crappy freighter, very low in the water – there was this great cheer that went up and everybody waved," said Hamilton. "It was really touching."

Hamilton was a little more resigned now than he had been previously about the general condition of the refugees. "They are in pretty rough condition. They have not had a bath in a month, or water – anything. It's really a bad scene. And, a lot of them have rashes." But the chances of a bath or shower for the first group of refugees prior to their departure for Canada remained out of reach.

Allen, too, had some of his own concerns about the reaction of the refugees when they finally arrived in Canada. "When you're talking to people on the buses, tell them that the military aircraft are being used only for the logistics of the thing," Allen instructed.

"It is not for any element of security, nor is any element of security implied in taking them to Longue Pointe military camp here," he continued. "It's just that facilities exist there for medical treatment and (immigration) processing. So they should not be alarmed that they're going into any type of camp."

Hamilton wasn't unduly concerned. "I don't think they're alarmed. I just think they're tearfully delighted."

The chaotic conditions under which the selection team worked were bound to have some repercussions. At 3 a.m. Friday, Hamilton discovered to his disbelief that the Canadians had not, in fact, selected 604 refugees. "We were 15 short." The error, said Hamilton, probably occurred when an application from a large Vietnamese family was processed twice.

"We had already told Ottawa that we had 604," said Hamilton. So, later on Friday he approached the Malaysian police with whom he had now developed a good relationship and asked them to take him back to the *Hai Hong*. He slipped away quietly, boarded a police launch and soon found himself alongside the old freighter. "I worked on my knees on the deck of the launch and processed 15 refugees."

As the reception team in Canada awaited the arrival of the refugees, they learned that efforts to find winter clothing in Kuala Lumpur had drawn a blank. The Red Crescent sweaters would help, but the people at Longue Pointe would now have their jobs cut out for them.

*The rusting Hai Hong carried 2,500 Vietnamese refugees.*

*Each refugee is believed to have paid 16 pieces of gold or $3,200 U.S. for a place aboard the squalid ship.*

*Refugees wait anxiously for news about their uncertain future.*

*The Canadian immigration team waits for refugees to arrive aboard a Malaysian minesweeper for interviews.*

*The immigration interview area aboard the Malaysian minesweeper Brinchang was rigged under an anti-aircraft gun.*

*Unlike small boats that carried refugees from Vietnam, the Hai Hong carried a large number of children and elderly people.*

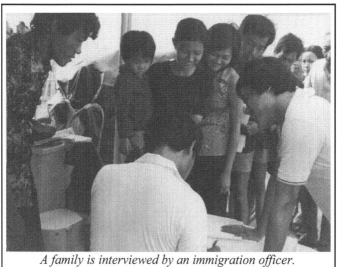

*A family is interviewed by an immigration officer.*

*A doctor examines a child.*

*The first Hai Hong refugee to set foot on Malaysian soil was a two-and-a-half year-old child, carried down a gangplank by Immigration Officer Ian Hamilton.*

*Hamilton was affectionately known as "Mr. Canada" by refugees at a camp at Pulau Bidong, Malaysia.*

*Photos courtesy of Ian Hamilton*

# CHAPTER SIX

# PREPARATIONS AT HOME

A number of things were on Bill Nauss' mind when the ad hoc task force met in the Bourque Building's second-floor boardroom in Ottawa on the eve of Cullen's November 18 announcement that Canada would take 600 *Hai Hong* refugees.

"We met to kick around some ideas," he recalled, particularly the elementary but difficult tasks of clothing, feeding and housing the refugees who would begin arriving in about a week.

Nauss began to jot down a few notes on a large pad, including a reminder that Longue Pointe military base had been used successfully as a transit centre in 1972 when chartered aircraft flew 4,420 Ugandan expellees to Canada.

The words "hangar," "deplane," and "clothing" appeared on the notepad. There would be a great deal of logistical work involved with the arrivals, he thought. "It was a question of these things having to be done and who was going to do them."

After the meeting, Nauss returned to his office and placed three telephone calls. The first was to Jacques Denault, Director of Immigration, Quebec Region, "to tell him what was on our minds." Denault's response was short. "No problem."

Denault was counting on two Canada Employment and Immigration officers to handle the job: Immigration Canada's Bob Lefebvre, who had organized the staging centre for the Ugandan movement; and Employment Canada's Thelma O'Connell, another veteran of the Ugandan operation. "We had people who had gone through this exercise before," said Nauss. "It certainly relieved me."

His two other telephone calls went to settlement officers André Pilon, Ontario Region, and Jim Pasman, British Columbia Region. "Whatever happened they'd be intimately involved" because of the number of refugees who would likely go to these destinations.

Nauss' military background – he was a major in the Ordnance Corps – began to filter through. The military's Mobile Command was at St. Hubert, close to a major Montreal airport. Longue Pointe, also near Montreal, had the housing facilities. "Things fell into place," and he recommended to Kirk Bell that DND be requested to provide Longue Pointe as the staging area.

Nauss, Bell, Allen and Hill met again on Sunday, November 19 when they discussed the possibility of having two staging areas. Bell spoke by telephone to Brigadier General Monty Wiseman to inquire about transport capability and to request facilities for staging centres at Longue Pointe and possibly London, Ontario. The military, said Nauss, seemed ready to go.

Then, after careful reflection about the idea of two staging areas, Nauss changed his mind. A centralized operation would be the best answer, and Longue Pointe the best location.

The one thing Nauss wanted to avoid was creating a refugee camp out of the staging area. As a former foreign service immigration officer, he had seen European refugee camps where some people had been residents for a lifetime. These people, he said, soon begin to lose their purpose in life.

"Just by the very action of being aboard the *Hai Hong* they (the passengers) were highly motivated and obviously strong-willed persons," said Nauss. He did not want to take the risk of keeping the refugees at the staging area too long and destroying their initiative. The refugees, he vowed, would remain at Longue Pointe no longer than a week.

While the physical well-being of the refugees was Nauss' prime responsibility, he also had some apprehensions about possible medical problems because there was only time to conduct cursory medical examinations of the refugees prior to their arrival in Canada.

"I was concerned that we might get people who would have to be hospitalized for long periods or kept in isolation," said Nauss. Medical treatment was one thing, but he worried about the impact that medical problems could have on public support if the public felt threatened. "I didn't want it (support) turned off."

Nauss was referring to the growing public support for the *Hai Hong* movement. Following the Minister's initial request for public assistance, Bob Douglas of *The Canadian Press* wrote a story on November 20 which triggered a flood of new inquiries from citizens who said they wanted to help in settling the refugees.

"The department is asking Canadians to inform employment offices or immigration centres if they are willing to provide help such as babysitting, housing and assistance in finding doctors," Douglas wrote.

Newspapers began to carry stories about reception plans at the local level. The Montreal *Gazette's* David Lisak wrote a story for the November 22 edition under the headline "Montreal Vietnamese ready to help when the boat refugees arrive here." Joe Serge of the Toronto *Star* reported November 23 that the "federal government and ethnic groups are lining up homes and jobs for the 200 refugees expected to start arriving in Toronto next week."

In Ottawa, Nancy McGee, Executive Director of the Ottawa-Carleton Immigration Services Organization, told the Ottawa *Journal* that 12 city agencies were mobilizing to receive the refugees and "generally make them feel welcome."

It soon became obvious to Nauss and other settlement officers that the CEIC could not take advantage of all the private offers. There were countless offers of furniture and clothing which posed storage problems, said Nauss. "Normally, we do not have storage facilities" and must rely on volunteer groups to provide space.

There was danger, he said, that the CEIC's lack of facilities and personnel to handle contributions of clothing and furniture could be counterproductive and discourage the public. The CEIC did not want to lose the goodwill.

This led Cal Best to send a telex to the regions on November 29 saying that "it would appear . . . we may be unable to take advantage of all the proffered assistance. Might I suggest that if this is the case in your region, you advise these persons of the continuing refugee program that includes a steady flow of

Indochinese refugees, that is: 70 families a month overall, and that their continued but longer term assistance would be most welcome in the months ahead." The same message was passed to the media.

Best said the current offers would be used "to advise officers overseas on where best to send other refugees whom they believe would require extra settlement assistance."

As the settlement people planned for the arrival, representatives of the Canada Employment and Immigration Commission, the Department of National Defence, Health and Welfare Canada, the RCMP and External Affairs met after lunch on November 20 to work out the operational plans to bring the refugees to Canada. General Wiseman noted that DND was still attempting to determine whether the military's Boeing 707s could be freed from current commitments to handle the airlift. The military, however, agreed in principle with the airlift, to be known as "Magnet."

Following the meeting, Best sent a telex to the Air Transport Board (ATB) to request permission to use military aircraft. "This request relates to the unknown health conditions of the refugees and the need to retain them in quasi-quarantine pending their medical examination/treatment after arrival in Canada," he said. The ATB's clearance came through the next morning.

Jack Manion, meanwhile, followed up his verbal discussion with C.R. Nixon, DND Deputy Minister, with a formal request for transportation. The Malaysians, he wrote on November 21, were permitting Canada to accept the refugees but the Vietnamese had to be transported from Malaysia immediately. "Unfortunately, the foreign commercial airlines have indicated to us their inability to carry those refugees selected by Canada."

By the end of that same day, DND confirmed that it could provide the aircraft. The Americans and Japanese had also agreed to allow the aircraft to refuel and change crews in Elmdorf, Alaska, and Yokota, Japan.

Two days later, the first military Boeing 707 left Canadian Forces Base, Trenton for Kuala Lumpur to pick up the first group of refugees.

# CHAPTER SEVEN

# AIRLIFT

By the time the first Boeing 707 completed the 9,000-mile flight to Kuala Lumpur, immigration officer John Almeida was beginning to feel as if he were "part of the aircraft's furniture."

He had been on the aircraft for 25 hours and watched as the crews changed at the refuelling stops in Alaska and Japan. "I came with the plane," he quipped, but was "glad to be the first one to go out."

Almeida had been working at his desk at the West Toronto Canada Immigration Centre a few days earlier when the Foreign Service, Canada Immigration, called for Cantonese-speaking immigration officers to accompany the refugees on each of the four flights to Montreal. Almeida and the three other immigration officers who responded – Charles Chow of Toronto, Y.P.G. Lau of

Winnipeg and Peter Chiu of Montreal – would be responsible for completing the immigration paperwork for refugees during the flight to Canada.

In Almeida's case, he made the flight on a round trip, non-stop basis, dubbing it his "70-hour adventure."

The temperature hovered around 32 degrees Celsius and the humidity was 100 per cent when the Boeing 707 arrived in Kuala Lumpur, Almeida recalled. "It really hit me hard. It was sticky. Just horrible." And, it was only 7:30 in the morning.

Malaysian police quickly surrounded the aircraft, noting that it was a military vehicle. "They wanted to search the plane to see if we were carrying guns," said Almeida. When the pilot explained "we do not carry guns," the police changed their minds but maintained tight security around the aircraft to guard against demonstrations.

It was another few hours before four busloads of refugees and a rented truck carrying their baggage pulled alongside the DND aircraft. The day had started before daybreak for the immigration selection team and the 159 refugees who would take this first flight. Hamilton and his team had left Kuala Lumpur at 5 a.m. to meet the minesweeper that picked up the refugees. The Canadians were not permitted to board the minesweeper while the *Hai Hong* passengers were being transferred, and Hamilton worried that substitutions might take place. He had issued Minister's Permits authorizing the refugees to enter Canada, but delivered them to Almeida so that they would not be lost, stolen or bartered aboard the ship.

Hamilton's attempt to obtain shower and bath facilities had been in vain but nature lent a helping hand. On arrival at the Port Klang pier for transfer to the buses, the refugees were caught in a torrential downpour.

Hamilton had warned Ottawa that the refugees "were not going to be a pretty sight." But they had done their best to look presentable and "given the circumstances they looked good but tired" when they arrived at the airport, Almeida said.

For the Vietnamese, the trip to the Kuala Lumpur airport marked the end of a 45-day ordeal. They were in good spirits as they settled into the aircraft, and burst into applause for Hamilton, Mullin and Martin.

Once in the air, Almeida began the arduous task of filling out forms and sorting out photographs. "They asked me a lot of questions," said Almeida, and when he made announcements over the aircraft's intercom system the refugees responded by clapping their hands. "It was their way of saying thanks."

Meanwhile, the refugees were not without medical assistance. New DND medical evacuation teams boarded the aircraft at each stop. Each team, consisting of a doctor, a nurse and two medical aides, "were very good," praised Almeida. "The refugees were re-examined after each stop," and there were few medical problems. One young child had a high fever and one woman was suffering from exhaustion.

Among the passengers on this flight was Luu who likes to tell the story of his first, yet puzzling impression of Canada. It was pitch dark when the Boeing 707 arrived at Dorval airport in Montreal. Seconds later, Luu and his friends were exchanging comments about a strange phenomenon.

"The sun was suddenly shining," he joked.

No one had told the passengers that the aircraft would enter a brightly lit Air Canada hangar.

# CHAPTER EIGHT

# ARRIVAL

The two key CEIC officers overseeing the operation at Longue Pointe were Bob Lefebvre and Thelma O'Connell, both of whom had previous experience in providing reception and initial resettlement services for the Ugandan movement in 1972.

Late Saturday night, November 25, Lefebvre and O'Connell watched from the sidelines as some 75 reporters, television camera operators and photographers vied for positions near the foot of the ramp leading to the rear door of the 707. The giant sliding doors of the sprawling hangar slammed shut, cutting down the chill that swept along the concrete floor.

A chartered bus, its doors open, was parked a few feet away from the bottom of the ramp, ready to welcome the new Canadians. Four ambulances stood by. Canadian reporters, joined by a few foreign journalists, waited eagerly for their first glimpse of the refugees. Their requests to accompany the refugees on the first flight from Kuala Lumpur had been turned down because of space limitations; and now the media w e r e asked to refrain from interviewing the Vietnamese on arrival to give them time to recover from their ordeal and orient themselves. Cullen and Couture decided against any formalities at Dorval, choosing instead to visit Longue Pointe a few days later.

The journalists began taking notes and snapping pictures as the passengers filed slowly down the long ramp. In spite of their long sojourn aboard the *Hai Hong*, the Vietnamese appeared to be in fairly good shape. And the Montreal reception was moving with military precision.

Richard Cléroux, writing for the Toronto *Globe and Mail's* November 27 edition, described the arrival and first full day at Longue Pointe.

*MONTREAL - The first planeload of 159 Vietnamese boat people arrived at Dorval airport just before midnight Saturday looking surprisingly rested considering they had just spent 30 hours on board the same aircraft.*

*The real surprise for military officials who welcomed them with warm blankets, handshakes and lollipops for the children came yesterday when it was discovered what huge appetites they had.*

*Some of them had been on board the ship, the Hai Hong, on its flight from Vietnam, overcrowded with 2,500 people for as long as 43 days. During this time they had had little food and not much more than rainwater to drink.*

*The aircraft, a military Boeing 707 which had stopped to refuel in Tokyo and Anchorage on its flight from Kuala Lumpur, was brought into a special hangar at Dorval where chartered buses were waiting to take the refugees to the military base in the east end.*

*There, a proper welcome had been prepared by Canadian Government and military officials as well as a delegation from Montreal's 8,000-member Vietnamese community.*

*The Government had people who spoke French, English, Vietnamese and Chinese, all languages spoken by the refugees, mainly middle class Vietnamese of Chinese origin whose ethnic background as well as their economic prosperity made them the object of abuse by the Vietnamese Government.*

*They were given new Canadian clothes, parkas for the adults, snowsuits for the children, socks, shoes and boots. Some had come off the aircraft barefoot, others wearing only sandals and pajama-type outfits.*

*One little girl struggled with a tuque, trying to figure out how to put it on using only one hand. Most had never seen snow.*

*Hand-lettered signs in Vietnamese had been up around the base to make things easier for them. Some public relations-minded Canadian official had given 5-year-old Tuyet Nga a Canadian flag which she waved as she stepped from the aircraft.*

*The welcome and immigration procedures took about three hours and they bedded down about 5 a.m. yesterday morning.*

*At 7 a.m., less than two hours after going to bed, the first of the refugees was at the door of the mess hall, looking for breakfast.*

*They came in and out all day to eat, one family after another, before returning to sleep.*

*"It's incredible that such little people could eat so much," said a bewildered warrant officer, André Houle, who is in charge of the mess hall. And he's a man who is used to feeding hungry soldiers.*

*Everything served to the refugees was eaten. They came back for more and what they couldn't finish, they'd scrape off their plates into doggie bags, tin cans, or anything handy around the kitchen, and take back to their barrack.*

*Some of them had spent as many as 43 days on board the refugee ship with very little food and nothing more than rainwater to drink. At one point they forcibly took the Indonesian crew's food and spent the final week without food until they were given some by the Malaysian Government.*[2]

The blueprint for the Montreal homecoming began when the Director of Immigration, Quebec region, Jacques Denault, called Bob Lefebvre to ask whether he could help with the *Hai Hong* operation. Lefebvre, on leave from his job as manager of the Jean-Talon Canada Immigration Centre, agreed to accept the demanding task as co-ordinator of the staging centre. He knew from his experience with the transit centre for the Ugandans that this would be a tough job with long hours.

Lefebvre's first call was to Major Raymond Dussault, Commander of Longue Pointe military base. They met to sort out their respective roles. Then Lefebvre started recruiting help from the CEIC's Quebec, Ontario and Alberta regions. He asked Health and Welfare Canada, Customs and Excise and Agriculture Canada to provide examination officers at Longue Pointe.

The military, said Bob Lefebvre, provided transportation, room service and 24 hour-a-day mess hall services as well as the barracks and other space. Employment Canada's Thelma O'Connell praised the soldiers who often carried the young and old so that they would not have to walk on the cold ground. "Those men were just extraordinary," she said.

One of Lefebvre's biggest problems was solved quickly by volunteers from the Vietnamese Association of

---

[2] Reprinted with permission of the Toronto *Globe and Mail*.

Montreal. "I needed interpretation services at the base," he said, noting that the main languages spoken by the refugees were Cantonese and Vietnamese. Only a few spoke English or French.

Lefebvre paid tribute to the Vietnamese Association and representatives of the Chinese community in Montreal, without whom "we would have had a mess." About 70 volunteers, many of them students who were refugees themselves in 1975, worked in shifts at Longue Pointe.

The Red Cross, meanwhile, volunteered to help at the reception centre, and arrangements were made to have representatives from the transportation companies on site so there would be no delays in sending the refugees to their destinations a few days after arrival.

O'Connell was planning to retire from her job with the CEIC at the end of the year and was attempting to clean off her desk when the call for help came through. "I was so pleased to have this last project as employment co-ordinator," she said. It meant that she could leave the government service "in a blaze of glory," she mused.

One of her tasks was to ensure that the refugees were properly clothed but, with the fast approaching deadline, she had little time to find a clothing store that could set up a shop at the staging centre. She made one call to Miracle Mart which had provided a clothing store during the Ugandan movement. "Are you ready to go?" she asked.

The answer was a prompt yes.

The clerks at the Miracle Mart store were mainly CEIC staff who were pressed into service, and armed only with checklists for clothing children, teenagers and adults. They would eventually outfit the Vietnamese at an average cost of approximately $160 per person.

The store's first brush with a shortage came early. The clothing had been stocked on the basis of general information telexes and manifests from Kuala Lumpur. Most of the shoes in stock were the wrong size. "It was three in the morning and Miracle Mart went to their warehouse to get the proper sizes," Lefebvre recalled.

Michael Prentice, staff writer for the Ottawa *Citizen,* caught some of the backroom happenings when he wrote November 27:

*The only hitch in the elaborate arrangements came while issuing clothing. "Some of them were pretty choosy about colours and styles," one military man handing out clothes said. "That's when the hold-up in the process came."*

As the refugees arrived at Longue Pointe they were given route slips to ensure they went through all the procedures. Families sat around large tables in the reception hall, waiting for immigration, customs and medical examinations, showers and clothing. Light food was served.

"Processing for the first flight took six or seven hours," said Lefebvre, mainly because "we had to clothe them completely." On subsequent flights, however, the clothing operation was streamlined and medicals were delayed because the refugees appeared in good condition. "Experience makes it perfect," said O'Connell.

Possible medical problems that had worried Nauss and other CEIC officers never materialized. Only a handful of refugees from each flight required special medical care or hospitalization, although ambulances at the airport were filled with people. Whole families would trek to the ambulances when one of their members was ill. They refused to be separated.

Some of the refugees developed scabies, an infectious skin disorder, but federal and provincial health authorities kept it under control. One teenaged boy required open heart surgery.

The new land and different customs would also have a traumatic effect on some of the older Vietnamese. Lefebvre remembers one case where an old man, seriously ill, was kept in hospital while his family moved on to their destination in Vancouver. "We had to send one of our people to visit him to calm him down."

Generally, however, families were kept in Montreal if one of their members was hospitalized. "We arranged to keep the families at the Y or at local hotels and looked after them," said Lefebvre. The military often drove family members to the hospital to visit.

# Chapter Nine

# Warm Welcome

As reporters gained access to the refugees for interviews at Longue Pointe, a tide of human interest stories and photographs spread across the country. Welcoming committees sprang to life in cities and towns as citizens eagerly awaited the arrival of their new neighbours.

O'Connell now faced the mounting pressure of moving the Vietnamese to suitable locations. "The Vietnamese are good workers" and are relatively easy to place, she said, but there would be little time to do extensive employment counselling.

"We did not want to keep people on the base for more than 48 hours because we had to make room for other flights" on November 28, and December 1 and 5, explained Lefebvre. The employment counselling was done on-the-spot, linking destinations with job orders that had come in from the regional *Hai Hong* co-ordinators, or with job opportunities in the regions. Other refugees were sent to live near relatives.

Some of the refugees worried about the weather in such places as Alberta, said O'Connell. "Many of them wanted to go to British Columbia because of the climate, but we had to counsel them to go elsewhere."

There was always a fine line to be drawn in the counselling process. "We had to convince the refugees that it was to his or her advantage" to go to a certain community, O'Connell noted. "At the same time, we had to be careful not to cause the person any dismay."

The employment counsellors worked quickly. On November 28, 11 families left the base in mid-afternoon for hotels in the Montreal area. Another family left that evening for Toronto. In less than two weeks the 604 refugees were moved: 16 to New Brunswick, 215 to Quebec, 229 to Ontario, 26 to Manitoba, 6 to Saskatchewan, 58 to Alberta and 54 to British Columbia.

On the political front a storm was brewing and was destined to erupt on the newspages. Alberta sent a telex to Cullen on November 21 in response to his request for provincial support in settling the refugees. Alberta said it would accept 50 of the new arrivals but added that it required federal guarantees on health, education, training and language costs for up to three years.

The ensuing publicity generated severe editorial criticism of the Alberta government. In an exchange of comments between Alberta and the federal government over interpretation of the telexes, Cullen decided to make them public to clarify the issue. Although the province eventually said it would take as many refugees as wanted to settle in the province, news about the offer was slow reaching the public.

On December 6, Cullen sent a telex to Reuben Baetz, Minister of Culture and Recreation for Ontario, after a story quoted Baetz as saying refugees destined for Quebec had received visas from that province and were handled differently than those refugees destined for other parts of Canada. "Those refugees destined for Quebec have not received Quebec visas or other special documentation," said Cullen. "Nor do the arrangements which have been jointly developed represent a form of creeping separatism. Rather they are derived from a Canada-Quebec Immigration Agreement signed in February of this year, an agreement which is considered by many to be a model of co-operative federalism. I would mention that the same terms, including selection abroad by provincial officers, were offered to all provinces."

Cullen said that in refugee matters "the federal government determines refugee status and all statutory requirements governing their admission. Quebec, in keeping with this agreement, has selected from the *Hai Hong* those refugees whom they consider can best establish in Quebec because of family links, language capability or general suitability."

Another round of warm human interest stories appeared in the local media as welcoming committees and reporters showed up at airports, rail and bus terminals to greet the refugees.

Refugee Luu, one of the first Vietnamese to enter Longue Pointe, was among the last to leave when the transit centre officially closed its doors at 4 p.m., December 8. He had written to Ernest Allen, whom he met on arrival in Canada on November 25, to say his arrival in Ottawa would be delayed because Major Dussault had requested his assistance as an interpreter. "It is very hard for me to refuse such a duty," he told Allen. "Furthermore, I would like to take this opportunity to contribute more efforts to serve our people."

Hamilton, meanwhile, was trying to "move heaven and earth" to fly Mrs. Luu and her six children from a refugee camp in Tajenpanang to Ottawa by Christmas. "They're just a marvelous bunch of people," he said.

On December 19, Ottawa *Citizen* reporter Rick Laiken witnessed a "tearful, joyful reunion at Ottawa International Airport," where Mr. Luu was embracing his family after their long separation.

When the Hai Hong operation ended, Cullen wrote to Ian Hamilton to express his appreciation for what he had done. "I was so impressed with Ian's contribution that I wrote to him to say that as a result of his work in this particular area and the splendid way in which he went about his job, the department stood a little taller in everyone's eyes."

Hamilton, affectionately called "Mr. Canada" by refugees at a camp at Pulau Bidong, Malaysia, continued to work at a gruelling pace for several more months – travelling from camp to camp in Malaysia, Singapore and Indonesia to process refugees for resettlement in Canada. When he returned to Ottawa in the summer of 1979 following a serious illness, the then Immigration Minister, Ron Atkey, presented him with a $2,500 merit award for outstanding service and contribution to the government's Indochinese Refugee Program.

The rusty freighter that brought the growing refugee crisis in Southeast Asia to the centre stage was put up for auction on April 1, 1981 by Malaysian authorities. But less than two months later, on May 24, 1981, the Hai Hong sprung a leak. It now rests on its side, waterlogged and unwanted, off the shore near Port Klang, Malaysia.

# EPILOGUE

The *Hai Hong* saga ended April 24, 1979, when the last group of 76 refugees from the ship left Malaysia for the United States.

Final resettlement by countries was as follows: the United States (897), Federal Republic of Germany (657), Canada (604), France (222), Switzerland (52), New Zealand (9), and Australia (8). [3]

The 604 refugees selected by Canada arrived at Dorval airport, Montreal, on four flights on November 25 and 28, and December 1 and 5, 1978; all were processed at the reception centre at the Longue Pointe military base by December 8. Their destinations in Canada were as follows:

---

[3] Source: United Nations High Commissioner for Refugees.

|  | Individuals | Families |
|---|---|---|
| New Brunswick Region | 16 | 2 |
| Quebec Region | 215 | 57 |
| Ontario Region | 229 | 52 |
| Manitoba Region | 26 | 5 |
| Saskatchewan Region | 6 | 4 |
| Alberta and NWT Region | 58 | 10 |
| British Columbia and Yukon Region | 54 | 10 |

When the refugees reached their destinations in Canada they received a great deal of support from local residents and gradually became established in their new communities. Some entered the labour force shortly after arrival; others took language training courses to improve their prospects for employment.

Meanwhile, the UNHCR was calling for greater resettlement efforts. The Canadian government responded by announcing it would accept 5,000 Indochinese refugees in 1979. By spring, there was another marked increase in the number of Indochinese arriving on foreign shores where they were not welcomed.

After the Liberal government was defeated by the Conservatives in the May 22, 1979 federal general election, outgoing Immigration Minister Bud Cullen urged his successor Ron Atkey to increase Canada's intake of refugees. The Canadian target was subsequently increased from 5,000 to 8,000 and Canadians were challenged to privately sponsor an additional 4,000.

In July 1979, as the human suffering in Southeast Asia increased to dramatic proportions, Canada expanded its program again by offering to accept up to 50,000 Indochinese refugees between January 1, 1979 and the end of 1980. The target would eventually be increased by 10,000.

The public environment in which the government launched the major 1979-1980 resettlement effort was marked by contradictions. On the one hand, public opinion polls showed that most Canadians were cool to the idea of increasing the number of Southeast Asian refugees coming into the country. On the other, media reports about the conditions faced by refugees in overcrowded camps abroad ignited a rash of editorials and criticisms of refugee interest groups about the speed and adequacy of Canada's response. Moreover, the media coverage had a catalytic effect in stimulating interest in a new and largely untested measure under the 1976 Immigration Act that allowed private sponsorships of refugees.

Evidently, the public's response in terms of material and volunteer help for the *Hai Hong* refugees, along with interest in private sponsorships, gave the government the political will to make a dramatic increase in the number of refugees that Canada would accept in 1979-1980.

Canadians responded to the challenge. Of the 60,000 refugees selected by Canada in 1979-1980, 34,000 were privately-sponsored.

"It was an extraordinary outpouring of concern and volunteerism across the country," reflected Michael Molloy, President of the Canadian Immigration Historical Society. "People from all walks of life put their beliefs and values to the test in a spirit of helpfulness and purposeful cooperation by providing financial support and by helping refugees to integrate into their new communities."

In total, more than 120,000 Indochinese refugees came to Canada between 1975 and 1994, making the movement the largest refugee resettlement operation in Canada's history.

The Hai Hong incident not only generated world attention to the festering refugee crisis in Southeast Asia, it was also the turning point for thousands of desperate people who found new homes in Canada and around the world. [4]

---

[4] In July 1979, when the UNHCR called on nations to expand their Indochinese resettlement efforts, 72 countries pledged to resettle 260,000 refugees in the next 12 months, double the original target.

# SUGGESTED READING

To mark the 40<sup>th</sup> anniversary of the fall of Saigon, the Canadian Immigration Historical Society and McGill-Queen's University Press will release a book in 2015, covering the Indochinese Refugee Movement 1975-1980.

The CHIS volume offers a fascinating look at how events unfolded for some 50 men and women who were on the front lines of Canada's biggest refugee movement in its history. The inside stories of these former government officers are rich in vivid accounts of the crucial factors that shaped their work: the squalid refugee camps and snake-infested jungles, the unique challenge of rapidly moving an unprecedented number of new immigrants half-way across the globe, and the operational task of delivering government-assisted and privately-sponsored refugees on schedule to their right destinations across the country.